LEMURIA

ISBN: 978-0-6151-4654-6

Printed in the United States of America.

LEMURIA

Debi Dipperstarlight

Acknowledgements

Thanks to

    Madeline Aldridge for reading the first drafts with love

    Candyce Hawk for the front cover, and for editorial comments

    Yuehua, for filling my days with delight and laughter

    And for Kehlana the Lemurian

Contents

The Lost Isle   1

Floral Worlds   9

Crystalline Realms   21

Mother Mountain   35

Dolphin Dreaming   47

Sea-flower   63

Weavers of Time   79

The Changing Times   87

Golden Rose   99

The Lost Isle

emuria, how your name has been forgotten over eons of time. Lost in the Blue Pacific, your landmass was hidden under an ocean of swirling tides. Pre-history has claimed not your name but different ones and the rest left lying for starfish.

Your cousin, Atlantis, the Isles of the West, was not so completely erased from memory. Another ocean bears its name. Atlantean memories resurface in esoteric literature and the bizarre happenings of the Bermuda triangle. You, Lemuria, forgotten for eons, are coming back in trickles of resurgence. There are those who remember your name and others who shudder with deep longing, when they hear the word, "Lemuria", whispered for the first time.

Mu, the Motherland, you were known as, more-or-less. Our language was like the rustle of leaves in a spring breeze, and the sounds have become solidified over time. Who is there to remember you now, to recall your glorious days in the sun? Why me, of course, writing this down, and you, dear reader, with dreams of your own.

Do your dreams leave you in an island in the sun, days of delight and adventure and nights of praying to the moon? Do you travel the faerie road in your imagination, thinking these beings the province only of children and the mad? Do you dream of days of peace when all grouped together in great councils of the wise, with no need for leaders or the criminally insane?

May you meet me here, in these pages of our lives, as your dreams intermingle with mine, and our crystalline records reverberate across millennium. For now is the telling time, the beginning of the Great Releasing. The Old Ways come again to the fore, the rest a bad nightmare, laid to rest.

Whence was Lemuria?

Archeologists and historians give timelines in stone, carbon dating, crosschecking, digging for dinosaur bones. The channels of Light give timelines as co-ordinates in space and time from the 7th dimension, or 8th, or 9th. Trust and feeling are the key to belief. Somewhere in between has come consensus.

Lemuria existed sometime BC, in the pre-dawn times of humanity. Throughout the ages, across the planet, images of Mu resounded. Some claimed Easter Island as yours; others said the isles of Japan, Hawaii, and the South Pacific. Those with memories long enough recall the last days of eruptions, when volcanoes spewed forth with all their might, and ash twinkled down, firelit, to earth.

For those who have forgotten, or simply weren't there to begin with, scientists provide useful insight. Geologists, anthropologists and archeologists, deep-sea divers and physicists all give account, in scientific format, of the probable existence of a long-ago island in the Pacific.

Where you went, old islands of Mu, nobody knows. Your people moved on, to other Earth places, to the hollow lands, to the worlds between time. But your body, Mother Island, your breathing earth, to whence and to where did it go when the Changes came?

All over the world there are hints of your heritage. Under the oceans, south of Japan, lie elegant temples, passages and tunnels and monoliths of stone. Hawaii contains oral traditions, handed down to today's people, of the great ancient Motherland. India has temples, pre-Hindu, which resonate with Lemurian energies. The matriarchal lineages in the islands of Bali are reminiscent of Lemurian ways. All this, of course, is not proof, but simply speculation and guess.

What can we say but a long ago island sank below the sea, it's sea-faring inhabitants escaping to far-flung lands. The ancient continent of Gondwanaland overlapped landforms that now constitute parts of Australia, India and Asia. Landmasses today are not the same as they were, and Earth is in constant change. Beneath the surface the continental plates slip and slide, bumping against each other, just short of an eruption. The monumental tsunami of 2004 brought hitherto submarine islands to surface. Could they have been mountaintops in Lemurian times? There is no way to say, with certainty. Landmass aside, it's certain, however, Lemuria is rising, if not the ancient islands, but in the consciousness of the people of Earth.

What does it mean to us, in these modern times, the declinations of an ancient, picturesque island? Lemurians were peaceful beings, society organized around goodwill and love. Conflicts were minimal, and resolved with grace. It has been suggested that the name of Earth's other great ocean, the Pacific, comes from Lemuria; that the ocean was so-named because of the peaceful peoples that had lived on it's shores.

How can anyone know, for certain, in the absence of archeologists and anthropologists, what the society of the Motherland was like? The answer to that question is where this tale begins. Two decades ago, I remembered my past as a Being of Light on the islands known to us now as Lemuria. Two years ago, I began to correspond with others who professed such memories. Many things in our recollections overlapped. Some recalled crystals and their use: specific crystals in specific places: and this matched my memories. Still others had stories to swap, stories which were very similar to each other's.

Imagine a tribe of children, from the same village, orphaned at birth or an early toddler age, sent to all corners of the globe after their village was destroyed. As adults, they start to correspond though the internet. They swap stories, flashes of images that had haunted them all of their lives. They tell of their humble beginnings in that long-lost village. Similarities begin to explode, stories, words and images matching those of others. Coincidence compounds into incredulity until the loose-knit clan start to speculate they may have all come from the same place.

Hidden records, held in a lost valley, suddenly come to light. It contains records of the events that led to the destruction of a village, on the other side of the mountain.

The records contain the names – and even more – fingerprints – of the babies and toddlers orphaned at the fated village. And the fingerprints match those of the people in the internet club, adults who have "never met", scattered in all parts of the world.

Sound improbable? Anything is improbable, until it's happened to you. And those hidden records exist. They are called the Akashic records, information stored in crystals and other planes that traditionally only Shamans or psychics of great renown even knew existed.

But that is not where our story lies. Outside, there is a crescent moon, shining yellow-gold in the hazy evening. That celestial sphere is still new, growing every day in small quantities of moonlight.

Crescent moon, so perfect in the night sky, come with us on our journey. Moon, will you be round and full when we've finished here, or waning, nearly gone, giving way to a new one again? Moon, golden moon and silver, new moon and old, stay with us through our tale, for we are about to delve right back... back... to the Beginning times.

Floral Worlds

My first memories of Mu came at a time when no-one much even talked about crystals. Ho! Is it possible such a time existed on Earth? How could we forget such things of importance, such valued and trusted friends? But forget we did, human beings lost to their heritage for millenniums. When memory first let its visions appear, I had to struggle to let them through.

I knew I did not look like "me", now, I didn't even look like a human. The body I inhabited in those long ago times was long, ethereal, transparent almost. It was not like the dense heavy physical matter that forms human beings today. It's lighter form made it easier to return to the pure form of spirit.

It was in this consciousness of spirit we made our descent downwards into the vibrant world of minerals, or floated softly into the faery world, accompanying those little winged Devas as they tended to plants and flowers. These times were those of spirit's first descent into the dimensional world. Everything was exploration, joy and delight.

Lemuria was seeded by the Star-beings, those who came to play on the new wonderland of Earth. We floated, rather than walked, our spindly spirit-bodies moving with the winds and the power of thought. We spent our time in ecstatic exploration of our new home. There were some who loved the plant world, with all its precious flowers and buds, and others attuned with the subterranean streams of minerals. Still others explored the waters, the gentle waves surrounding our island home, communing with the dolphins who had come to play.

My first emergence in the natural world was to commune with the vibrant dancing nature spirits. For Lemuria was a green place, a green, loving place. Abundant fruit, beautiful people, streams and rockeries that sang. Birds – the most glorious birds of vibrant hues – sang songs, a joyful message. Lemuria, a tropical mansion with crystalline magic, was indeed a heaven upon earth.

I had to struggle to remember it. Like many others presently incarnated upon Earth, I was sure I'd been on Atlantis. Beyond that, I had a memory of another place, a green island. In my mind it was slightly to the northwest of my home in Australia, and east of where Atlantis had been... and long submerged. The island didn't show up on any maps then, at the time of my first memories.

But what a peaceful, beautiful place! It seemed to me to emphasize all that Atlantis wasn't. No trickery, no fights, no false democracy, no going against well-established principles for individual gain ... indeed, no concept of individual gain. Everything was in harmony. The nature spirits were our best friends. We were in communication with them all of the time. They were playful, joyous entities, and they made the leaves breathe deeper and the flowers bloom in richer array.

Our flowers were very special. Because we communed with them regularly, we'd been given the privilege of entering their floral world. From deep inside their structure we saw their colour and their shapes as they unfolded to the world, blessing the sky and drinking from the Earth.

I am a structure of atoms, which informs this dance of unfolding. I bloom as my matrix impulses me; I lift out of the tight bud slowly. I have soft petals, which fold over my sleeping smoothness. I feel warmth – great warmth – so I awake. Quickly now, I let all the petals of my loose body stretch and unfold to the sun. I am a gift to those entities who walk and fly and crawl. I am a pleasure of sight and smell for the moving ones. For some, a pleasure of sound, too. Amongst the moving ones, not all can hear my subtle song.

As we communed especially with flowers, the floral kingdom and our consciousnesses decided to blossom new kinds of beings. We, the Lemurians, would meld with the plant consciousness and collectively determine the shape and form, the characteristics, of a new breed. We were not scientists analyzing molecular structures of plants. We were not farmers grafting one bit of this onto one bit of that. We were consciousness, we were dancers on the breeze with the leaves of trees, we were creators, and we built the idea of new species of flowers along with the existing flowers and plants themselves. We were privileged invites into a secret world. We strode with ease across vast sections of countryside, and laughed with the flora along the way.

We created tulips, and roses too. We were pleased and content when the butterflies danced amongst our floral tribute. We were exalted when the butterflies drank our flower-juice. We were excited when the sharp beaks of birds delved into our private recesses, and lapped up our moist secretions, our sweet honey.

Fairies and devas flew about, little puffs of brightness and light. Although small, their gentle vibrations were wondrous and they held the matrix of their chosen plant's formation gently, skillfully, with delight. As I had first written those words, I was dancing around my garden, talking to the devas, making flower essences with pure water and sunlight. Today, flower essences have become a recognized and popular mode of healing, thanks to the pioneering work of Dr Bach who first made the flower essences, now named Bach Flower Remedies.

There were others who preferred to mediate with the trees, who became stubborn, brown, immobile things with their roots crawling down to rocks and stone. Others talked to fairies and elves, who felt more comfortable with these flighty spirited beings. We all came together at times, when we'd report on our progress, our ideas, and our playful exploration of our dimensional paradise. The flower people would report the idea of a new flower then how they planned to seed it. There would be technical information involved. The mineral-lovers would discuss their sojourns beneath the living soil, report upon their concerns and ideas of the mineral kingdom.

Those who worked with the flower world spread their consciousness thin but lengthy over the wide ground. They could feel the flower-tops sway in the breeze, and felt great tears of pain when an animal galloped over their fields, flattening the plant life in its wake. In latter days of Mu, the beings who had taken on more substantial human form would wear garlands around their neck, lovingly picked and worked into leis with the very spirit of the flowers themselves. For the flowers, they took on new life, not dying as they were picked but transforming partially their plant-world consciousness into the awareness of a striding being. The garlanded flowers began to feel, in little gulps of awareness, what it was like to stride over the land which was their body, their mother. When Mu sank her body under the sea, her inhabitants, some of them, went to Hawaii and the lands of the South Pacific, where floral necklaces still abound.

Roses, the pure expression of the floral world, were created by impression in Lemuria. In those times, so much was co-creation, imagining a beauteous expression of the world and then creating it. All around us was beauty, as we lived in a tropical world. Giant hibiscus bloomed naturally on the hills; frangipanis populated the valleys and gave off fragrance in the evening breeze.

We wanted a new flower, a complete expression of natural beauty. The Queen of Flowers, the one who expressed the pure light of the heavens on this new world of earthen grace. We sunk into the light of our soul-races, and sought guidance from our stellar homes.

We asked the greatest truest Source of light to enter our mediations and dreams. We communed with the fairy devas, and asked for their expert guidance. And we were drawn to the high hills were the wildflowers grew.

Small delicate things, we saw, these flowers on the islands in the colder climes. On bushes and hedges they grew, in rambling profusion, and their petals enfolded over each other in pure simplicity of grace. Small pink blossoms covered the green growth in gay profusion. Ahha! Someone dreamed the Rose, a larger, gentler, more exquisite version of this wildflower, then another dreamed it, and another, till the perfect vision was implanted in our minds. We told each other of its beauty, this magnificent Rose, not by drawing it in the sand or the subtle parchment made from dried grain stems, but by sending it's image to each other's dreams.

Finally we communed. Each held it's image, the flower of our uttermost dreams, in our hearts till finally the

Drawer drew it. She held a stem of a long bloom, into which she had breathed the fluid of indigo. Ink seeped from out of this pen made of flower-stems. From her magic hands and onto the parchment, an image of the Rose appeared. A collective gasp emerged: so perfectly had she captured our own desires.

The Rose was of Earth and of Heaven. It's predecessor had grown here, naturally, the rambling rose, a wild-flower of heady scent. And in the Star systems, from whence we came, many had a memory of a Rose-like flower. For perfection it was, in the floral kingdom. We attuned to the magnificent and complex universe of Form. We collected the wild roses and breathed in their scent. We choose many soils and melded them, till a perfect soil emerged, rich in nutrients.

Then we joined in holy communion, with all that was and will be. All That Is blessed us with galactic joy, and out of our bliss, our Rose emerged. We planted the old seeds and blessed them with grace. We watered them with water from the purest stream. We asked for the Flower of our Dreams to emerge.

One fine morning in the wee hours of dawn the Day's Keeper cried out for all to come: Hoorah! It had bloomed, and the bud was magnificent. A deep rich red was hidden in the large bud. We were delighted with it's size, much richer than the wild-flowers. We had filled the soil with so many nutrients and watered the roots with the purest of spring water. We had blessed its growth with our love and meditations.

We kept watch as the day bloomed in perfect sunlight. Slowly she opened her petals. Such bliss is hard to describe, from the world of today, so tainted with doubt and cynicism. Yet the long-ago times had no such concepts, only love, only joy, filled our every days. Sink into the beauteous vision of the flower as she unfolded to the morning sun! Watch as she lifts up her head to the skies, loosens her silken petals, and opens to a brand new day.

What beauty it was! We called for a council and all came, seated in concentric circles around our new joy. We called her Rose, the Rose of Tralee. This Celtic name is all that is remembered of the long ago Lemurian Rose. Tra-le-le, and Tra-le-la, a song of joy to all hearts. The memory still held in the celtic lands, and roses kept traces of faint echoes of the once glorious times of Mu.

A Rose, a rose by any other name, she entered our poetry throughout the eons, her flower coming to symbolize love and joy and all that's pure. For thus She was birthed, in love and joy, in the ancient times, whence the World was once new. Lemuria, you gave us so much, leaving traces of your bliss down through the ages. Who could have thought your gifts so great, who could imagine your once presentient grace could live still, after so long buried in pre-history?

The Rose was held as the perfection of all flowers, and we put her gorgeous form in our temples and gardens. Our Lemurian world was perfected by this perfect of all in the floral realms.

Crystalline

Realms

At a particular time in a particular space, I left my beloved flowers to sink deeper into dense earth. I'd slide, softly, along the topsoil, following the roots of the plants as they searched for water. I'd commenced with this living, submerged kingdom, as root structure, where underground vines of a thousand species curled and twined together, sharing their bright consciousness. Yet rather it was like one living, breathing organism, whose parts were made of the roots of plants, which, in their above-ground expression, appeared as separate entities and species.

We, the Lemurians, knew different. We, the people of the faery kingdom, knew underground was all a living oneness. We had deposited our consciousness amongst the roots and vines, and emerged to tell the story. We of the Plant people knew how to breath with the leaves, drink with the roots, hold firm ground like the trees. We regularly conversed with Plant Devas, those beautiful faerie spirits who lived with the Plant Kingdom, guiding its growth.

All areas in our garden were for pleasure and exploration. We respected the living truths of all entities and were gentle in our relations with them. Perhaps, as individuals, we had a particular inclination to one aspect of our planet, like I had with my flowers, but that did not stop us exploring other areas. Indeed, it was almost required – as much as requirement could be said to exist amongst our gentle people – that we venture our consciousness into all areas. We were here to explore the dimensions of the physical world, and explore we did.

I sent my consciousness down below the ground, far below the roots of the tallest trees. I'd gone underground originally to follow the roots of the plants and to explore their source of nourishment, but now I was going further, much further. Beyond surface rock and into the hidden layers, down I went, into the silent recesses of earth. Oh, how beautiful our planet was then, the precious underground labyrinths.

If the plant kingdom had formed on floating, dancing consciousness, breathing in the air, drawing on earth's substance and blossoming her Beauty, then the Mineral kingdom.... O the brilliant radiance of mineral life was beyond speech. Deep under dark earth, beyond the fetid mulch of autumns and winters past, past the steady grey layer of granite, was such a bedazzle, such a spectacular series of crystalline matrices... Who could begin to describe its adventurous wonders?

I was captivated. Mesmerized by the exquisite, exotic beauty, I rarely surfaced for air. My body began a slow hibernation while I, spirit substance, danced around ruby rockeries and crystal corridors. I joined a group of "crystal-pullers' who "pulled" crystals out of the ground by mediation. I immersed myself in this work and play. (We had no such division. We simply danced the joyous currents of life, delving deeper into the mysteries of the dimension physical.)

We would convene at a spot where one of our group had seen a particular crystal cluster underneath the ground. Some others would follow, to inspect and observe. Having confirmed that this was of a particular quality beneficial for the world – suitable for healing or for meditation, or simply to explore and learn from, the group would meet on the same spot, join consciousness and meditate, imploring the governing consciousness of the crystal group to send us one of their kind.

Sometimes the response was rapid, as if the crystals were bursting of their own accord, with the desire to surface and contemplate the bright, sunny day. At these times, the crystals that appeared in their bright plentitude quickly paired off with a human partner to mutually explore the realms of consciousness.

Mostly, however, the crystals took some time to rise from their subterranean arena and face the bright light of day. With each mediation they would rise a bit further, changing the course of their underground structure. It was, of necessity, a slow process, as we could not disrupt the underground systems substantially. We did not wish to cause serious problems to the metabolism of Earth, so we waited, slow patient times, for the crystals to emerge in their own glorious heartbeat. Always, we allowed for the underground structures to gently reshuffle and solidify, as the crystals began their surface upward.

On some occasions this process took years. We began to learn the pace of various structures – different minerals could travel though differing substances at different paces. We learnt which rocky natures, what sediments in the garden, offered a smooth passage to which kinds of rising crystals, and which elements caused a slowing down or cessation. We became experts at estimating the time needed to "pull" many different crystal groupings out of the ground. It was such absorbing work, that we did little else. When the crystal eventually rose and was released from earth's bosom, it was up to the original person who had suggested it's release, along with those who'd travelled the underground corridors to participate in it's observation, to decide how best to interact with the crystal.

Healing, music-making, functioning as a living library, space-travel, planetary alignment, sooth-saying, future-telling, past-seeing, heating and cooling... all of these and more were potential ways the crystals might be worked with. It was rare – no, never, that a crystal was used simply for jewelry. The concept of jewelry means something that is worn purely to adorn the body, to enhance the physical appearance. Our crystals, although often placed on the physical body, were never there simply for adornment. There was always a purpose.

To heal, to enhance the operations of a particular organ or function of the body, to assist communication with far distant others, to gain access to designated places (opening doors by vibrational alignment), to function as recorders for special events, to give the wearer information of a particular kind, to assist in dreaming, astral travel and soul-travelling, telepathy... the list goes on. To enable the wearer to flow between realities. To enable the wearer access to diverse communities upon earth. To enable the wearer to fluctuate, back and forth, along time-lines. The crystals were our treasure and we loved them with all our souls. To my Lemurian consciousness, mining for minerals was not only insult added to injury, but plain stupidity.

I remember one particular cat, a light, silk-coated sleek black cat, with the most remarkable oval opalescent eyes, who was drawn into a matrix of shining quartz. She loved this crystal, and would caress it and stroke it, rubbing her feline body along its smooth edges, purring all the time. We even changed her name, nicknaming her "crystal cat"!

Animals, like people resonated to particular crystals. Some of us who worked in the Mineral Realms excelled in the skill of matching people – or even animals - to their resonant crystals. This precious work was done by simply attuning to the energy of the crystal. It was the crystalline energy, always, that chose it's human companion, the human beings of the Mineral realm acting only as conduits for the gem-matrix's consciousness. By simply being with the crystal, the matchmaker would attune to its energies, and, with an emergence of clear vision, would see the human to which the crystal was best suited. Many crystalline and human matchings were done in this way. If

28

someone was called to a particular crystal, she would often first discuss it with the matchmakers, who understood the energies more than others. Yet if the crystal called, and a human heard its cry, more than likely that crystal was to be matched accordingly. Nothing prevented someone from simply picking up a crystal that had emerged on their path, and bringing it to their home. The matchmaker's role was to further deepen the understanding of the crystalline connection.

Those days of delight and wonder! The crystalline world shone bright and true. Willingly they surfaced, the crystal ones, to lie shining on the ground of the fairies. If someone passed their way, they would acknowledge it, and ask it to whence it wished to go. Perhaps the stone was to accompany that passer-by on his journey for a while, perhaps it was meant to be left there, lying in the sun.

In the great distant fields there were those who built a house of pure crystalline vibration. Like ice its walls stood, sacred and shining in the sun. Its dimensions were such that it was enough for most to contemplate its richness from outside, marvelling at the way it shone in the rays of our golden sun. Other beings, pure as floating droplets of water, ventured into its hallowed halls. Inside light shone with a magic dance of rainbows. Light beams of every hue made spaces and places of delight. Children especially loved to come here to play, for theirs was the kingdom of spontaneous joy.

Across the halls of time we come again to be re-acquainted with our Lemurian kindred. Lemurian crystals abound once more on our earth. Constrained by the demands of our time, they are usually surfaced by rough mining, the whirring of machines accompanying their journeys to the surface planes of earth. Despite the severity of these mechanical sounds on their precious vibrational structures, the crystals line up to ascend to the top. They too wish to be united with their Lemurian brethren and their sister-kind from the ancient days. Their magnanimity is astounding: willingly they suffer being pulled and prodded, so they may again commune with us and share their knowledge.

Crystals, you are called by differing names: Lemurian seeds, the crystal skulls, Lemurian lasers and wands. What matter it? The names you are given are not the same as before, yet they suit the demands of the *now* time. Come you have to light our way again, as we return, slowly, steadily, to the ways of old.

Lemurian magic, you are in our dreams every night. As we set our crystals on makeshift altars, as we bathe them in the light of the moon and stars and sun, we are remembering the ways of old. Soon we will dive down again, precious kindred, and assist your emergence in the old ways. Soon you will no longer feel the harsh cold of steel against your bodies. We will send our fingertips into the mud and earth, and emerge with your beauty, oh crystals of joy.

The brightest of you all, the most perfect in geometrical symmetry and Light reflection, was the diamond. Like Roses to the floral world, diamonds were the Perfection of the mineral realms. And like the rose did, Diamond, you merged from the perfect purity of our hearts. In love with the clear radiance of quartz, we merged with its consciousness to form and fathom the mineral response to heavenly perfection. Over geometric fissures and the false landscapes of time, we watched you merge under geo-palatial pressure. We travelled the sinuous highways that few could follow: the snake-light flowings of time. From our hearts you emerged in the distant times and we observed your grace and were in wondering gratitude.

Ah! Who could believe such tales now? So few have recalled their own grace, they doubt that of others. This tale, dear sister, dear brother, is not mine: this tale is YOURS! Yes yours. For you too helped this beauty to be!

You keep Diamond here by your belief if it's grace. For if you did not believe it, how could it be? It would disappear with the mermaids and unicorns, that most pure of animals who comes from the diamond essence. White as snow, as pure as children's tales, the Unicorn enters our imaginations as some improbable tale of mystery.

And the Diamond? Oh, that's REAL, you say, for you have seen it. Oh? Have you held it in your hands? Oh? You wear it on your fingers? You believe in it's reality as it's facets strike the sunlight every day and send of beams of love to your heart. What is reality, though, but what is in your mind and hearts and that which you choose to perceive. If you perceived the Unicorn, would she become real? If you heard her distinct footsteps with your physical ears, would you then say she "exists" and thus is "real"?

I will not say Unicorns existed in Mu. My tale is about diamonds, and you can see them. Are not they perfect? Do you not desire them? Do your womenfolk love to have them on their rings, symbols of eternal love? Diamonds emerged in the Pure Light of the Universe, a geophysical response to the Light-codes of the creational matrix.

Diamonds and Roses, we held you in loving perfection and preferred to express our awe at your majesty in your natural, original form. After crawling through complex subterranean tunnels, we viewed the diamantine glories, shining in underground caves, lighting the darkness by sheer presence. Some small portions fell of the walls; we took those ones, and those ones only, in gratitude, and crawled back along the corridors of time to our own thence. These pieces we put by the temples on Mother Mountain, and one large beauty, we used to propel a ship. And the Roses, we placed those which left the bushes in grace upon our altars, and planted seedlings everywhere in our gardens. The perfection of the mineral and floral realms were out most revered treasures.

Mother

Mountain

Vibrating noticeably as it sat on an over-hanging ledge at the top of a sheer rock was the central – in fact the only – ceremonial object in the large cavernous temple. Lit dimly by phosphorescence, the large cave was nonetheless bright enough to see by. Around the edges of the outcrop where the crystal sat, little fairy lights gave of a warm glow. Those who wished to focus their thoughts, soothe tangled emotions, or simply commune with its majestic presence, would sit cross-legged on the cave floor in front of the Ruby Crystal.

The natural golden aura of the caves, the fairy lights surrounding the crystal, and it's own supreme radiance, gave enough light to observe the crystal and to navigate inside the cavern. Adepts took turns at bathing the crystal with pure spring water and taking her out into the sunlight and moonlight to recharge her energies. Those with sight –

as most Lemurians had – could see red beams of light emanating from her when she stood in certain locations under the noon sun.

On solstices and equinoxes, we would stand in geometrical formation, as the angle of the sun hit the crystal atop a toll or hill, and the Ruby Light would channel outwards, along the lines marked by the Energy Keepers, the people who stood on her lines of Light. The Energy Keepers, neither priestesses nor scientists nor leaders of the community, but people simply in tune with the crystal who may have come from those occupations or other types of professions, were to do what their name indicated. Absorb the bright sun-enhanced rays of the Ruby, and keep those vibrations flowing, in simple sublime radiance, out to those lands and people who were not afforded to be in her direct presence. That was the responsibility of those who stood bathed in Ruby light.

By this time, Lemurians had solidified into a more human-like body, though taller, thinner, and less dense than today's humans. The early Lemurians had more spirit-like, ethereal form. In order to further fully experience the Planet of Gaia, we densed up, by the power of thought and manifestation.

With a more solid form, it was difficult to travel freely,

like we had in our taller, thinner manifestations. Then, it was simply a matter of rearranging our molecules by thought, and easy enough to slide through matter. The denser form made traveling a tad difficult. We had to learn to maneuver such bodies. It was like the astronauts, for the first time on the moon, no doubt. We giggled and laughed as we learnt how to walk with such heavy suits, and had to invent new ways to pass where before we could have gone with ease.

The entrance to the cave was controlled by an energy–enhanced door. Standing before it, one had to state one's intentions. A remote, telepathic controller would then open it. Entering into the subterraneous world was like entering into a new existence. Underground was not the same as above, the very structure of matter seemed changed. Once inside, somehow, we seemed able to revert to our lighter state, and float around the cave as before. To this day, I don't quite understand how that magic occurred.

Floating consciousness, Beings of Light and Love, had merged with the ruby, strengthening her powers, giving her greater jurisdiction. Her energies could be felt far across the islands. Inside the cave, it seemed nothing had changed. The old world was the same as the new, and time stood still inside.

There were many other caves we would visit, used for many different purposes. Some were temples, some were homage to the seeding stellar races, and some were for food storage. There were other caves that were underwater, and we had to swim to reach them. I remember Levethias. His name sounded something like that. He could swim like no-one else we knew. From the shores we would watch him go, disappearing underwater for seeming eternities, then rise, glorious, for breath. It was hard for me to see him, with my eyes as they were, so far away, but when he returned and emerged from the sea his body glistened with salt and sea-spray.

He would swim unaided, underwater, to far-away islands. He would go to the beautiful island of the mountain. One singular mountain, lavender in the distance, rose up from the beaches. Around it were tropical vegetation, palms and fruit trees, and large fronds of ferns swayed green and gentle in the breeze. Shaking the water off his body he walked the path to the mountain's base. It was too far to see with our normal eyes, of course, but those of us in his family were able to look through his eyes. Older sister made a speaking commentary, for those without direct connections to his sight.

Alone he walked, till he came upon the mountain. Bowing, then dropping his body to green earth with his eyes on the beautiful peak, he summoned his energies, made his greetings. *Mountain Mother, I bring you greetings from the people of Mu, from the distant island across the seas. Mother Mountain, I bring you gifts.* He took off the shell hanging around his neck, and placed it on the earth beneath him. *Mother Mountain, this shell is from our lands. We bequeath it to you, and so now, as in the past, and all our futures, we are connected. With this shell Mother Mountain I ask to reconnect and strengthen our old ties. Send your wisdom and strength to our people who wait on the shore, and watch with me.* A thousand eyes became visible through him. Our eyes, those of us tied to him via family blood or bonding, momentarily fluttered in the distant space. This I saw with my connecting eye. Older sister continued, channeling his words and mimicking his movements.

He drifted, as if he were floating, across to the place where Mother Mountain rested her heavy body on earth. Close up the rock seemed not lavender but glistening silver. A small hole was visible. Levethias bent down and began chanting. As a one, those on the beach began chanting too. We sang the words, we opened our hearts. We kept the

41

chant sacred and sweet as Levethias crouched and slunk through the small opening. His body seemed elongated as he squeezed through.

On the other side of the hole he emerged into a grand wide garden. Above him like us was the blue sky and sun. It was a dimensional illusion. From the beach we could see only sheer rock. From Levethias' vantage point right before the mountain, the front face of the mountain seemed to be one solid rock. Only by crawling through the tunnel, did the garden appear, and another face of the mountain, lavender bright in the sun. It was magic each time. Levethias had swam to the island many times, to give reverence to the Mother Mountain, and each time, as he surfaced from the small tunnel, a hush overcame those of us watching and listening through Older Sister's commentary. For those of us with sight, by virtue of being part of Levethias' family, it was a breathtaking vision. The garden was grand and glorious. Sunlight shined on everything. Fairies darted around the bushes. One great luminous rock, the baby of Mother Mountain, stood bathed in golden sunlight. Levethias greeted the baby as he always did. He placed his hand above it, and then, as if waiting for some unseen signal, placed his hand on top of Baby Rock. *Greetings, Baby Mountain, from the people from yonder island. One day you will be a glorious mountain, like your mother. The people of yonder island send you their greetings.* And then, the part I always loved, Levethias returned to his original spirit body and melted into the substance of Baby Mountain. Emerging the other side, he turned, placed his hand on Baby Mountain in thanks, and continued his journey,

Ah, such wonders of the ancient times. These things today seem the stuff of fantasy and clever stories. Yet then, our families were never separate. We were one, melded together in ways difficult to imagine today. So much forgetting has taken place. The very name of our Mother, lost for so long. Her name not once yet thrice lost though the eons, Earth, Terra Firma, Tierra .... Gaia as a living, breathing, magnificent being had been lost in the human mind.

Yet now her name has resurfaced, triumphant. Now she is free to be herself again. Gaia, what a wondrous being of immense beauty. What incredible treasures you hold on your shore. Gaia, the humans have not cared for you as we should, but we are learning again now, Gaia, our Mother. After eons of fortitude, you now raise your seas. Your temper flaring in spontaneous earthquakes. You shake, a planetary shudder, and dismiss all that does not honour you. Gaia, our Mother, you have had enough. You rise again now in all your celestial dignity, you are transforming with us into the new world.

There are those beings existent on your surface who have always honoured you, Mother Gaia. They are the ones humans turn to, in need of love and spontaneous gaiety. They are the swimming ones, the delightful ones, the dolphins. Who is not immune to their charm, their seeming simplicity as they play in the waves? The old, the young, people from the shores of the new world and old, all countries, all creeds, without distinction, honour and love you, dolphins. The most hardened of hearts cannot fail to be drawn to your magic, dear dolphins swimming in our oceans, and those hardened hearts find smiles emerging on their lips when they see you at play.

For so long you have graced our earth, with your Elder cousins, the whales. Back in Lemuria, we were glad to have you with us, sharing the joy of our new earth. You came, as we, from the stars to bless the waters of Gaia. You played and sang. Dolphins, your songs kept the gradients flowing smoothly, your singing kept the oceans at peace. Even though humans forgot your abilities, we never forgot your grandeur, and your enormous compassion. As children we heard tales of how you like to help people. Across many cultures these tales came. And into our own dreams you slipped, dolphin friends.

Dolphin

Dreaming

In times of Lemuria, dolphin temples abounded. There were some underwater ones, built of flowers and flowing rocks, and the famous one above the seas on the island to the left of the big island. From the top of the rock we'd see the dolphins dancing in the water. I see them in a circle now, a magic dance of the sea and wind. They were drawn to that sun-blessed spot in the ocean, and we, the fuller-bodied people now, watched them, swam with them, learnt their melodious songs.

How times had changed. If I look down on the then me, I have a body, a slim tall one. I would look much like an extra-tall present day human. It was the days of later Lemuria and we had "densed up", taken on human-like form. There had already been some cracks in the earth and warnings of what was to come.

But I haven't reached that point in my tale yet, so I will

go back to the dolphins cavorting in the sun. The groups of friends in the water were such strong swimmers and so adept at aqua-batics, they almost seemed like the dolphins themselves. I had taken part in the communion many times, but today I am sitting on the great peak watching them play together. My friends were both human and dolphin: we knew them as sisters and brothers of the sea. They taught us many secrets of their home world, great stretches of blue and beyond, blossoming as endless waves upon our shore.

As our forms had densed up, less time was spent entering the Realms as we had in earlier times. We had jobs to do, houses to build, food to find. Travelling into the faery dimension, the devic kingdom and the endless mineral gleam, was not as natural as before. It was thought to be done as a special technique, as a method of learning and studying. When spirit left our physical bodies we flowed through the joy of crystal and danced with the faeries as ever playful: but this was no longer our continuous state, as now we had denser bodies to take care of. Clans formed along groupings of old. Leaders of a sort emerged, queens and priestesses and town councilors.

Ah! But the dolphins! I'm getting bogged down in history and there they are, still at play. Dolphins of old, what do you have to tell us today? That your ears hurt, from the sonic boom? That your sisters are imprisoned by the evil of the world? Your brothers kept like guard-dogs by the military, your cousins forced to perform in aquatic circuses?

Yet still with glee you dance your tune, always and ever across the world. You give your grace without a second thought, your smiles of love a jump up for air. What then were you, to us, dear dolphin? Companions you once were, of the ways that shone. Companions to dance in this the new world, watery beings of laughter, quick to travel through the warp of time, to other worlds from whence you came.

Dolphin Elder, would you speak now?

Indeed I do, Sister of the East.

What would I record of your words, Wise One?

That we come to dance again with you, the human ones.

That we come again in droves to the planet we nearly left, so polluted the waters, so harsh were the waves. But we have felt the light touch beauteous Gaia's face, we have seen her radiant in the Universal Mind, we have seen the Grids lift, all silvery sparkle, we have heard the first of Gaia's sighs of bliss.

Again we come, from the space of old, transitting through the dimensions of time. We will repopulate your seas in honour of Gaia, Great Goddess beyond your imagination. She so enormous in her disposition of Grace, she so blessed and beloved of all heaven.

We come again to sing to Gaia, to awaken the treasures in all her pores, to commune as one in the infinite seas, the wide blue heaven that to us is the Oceans. You will see us come back, hesitantly at first. Your newspapers will be full of stories. Photographs will show children riding on our wild backs, safe seas will delight with hordes of us!

Slowly you will lose all your fears, even those amongst you who choose not to believe. Those ones we especially seek out, in love: the hurt ones of close-d minds. They will be drawn to the beaches and see us in their dreams, such is the power of our manifest ways. For now we are free to be as we are, messengers from another realm. All will see this, and nod in accord. For Gracious Gaia has given us such joy. Her atmosphere tingling with presentiment bliss:

Only now is the heaven created on earth.

We have come to play and commune of old. Excitement washes through our starry realms, as we line up to descend into mortal Earth again. We are expectant with love to enjoin with you, we can hear your whisperings in our dream.

You call us so often, so many of you. We are so proud you choose us, our race, as your confidants. We are honoured to offer you our joy abundant. Swim with us in the turquoise sea. Come now to our playground, we await your grace.

Some other time, I had a dream. Let me recall it. In the river, I'm swimming. A dolphin jumps up. She is plump and curvy and pink majesty. I watch the pink dolphin of the Amazon cavort and turn, her bottle-nose pointing upward to the sky as she jumps. She is beautiful and gracious, and seems to be talking to me.

She greets me in dolphin song: a tune of joy and beyond. I smile back and behold her pink-skinned beauty. It's not pig pink, nor pale pink, nor even grey-pink. Its dolphin pink! .... a kind of skin colour.... She jumps up high and then is splashing in the river. I'm down underneath the waves with her and she nudges the waves with her nose.

I'm somehow riding with her, but at the same time I'm not.

Then she calls me sister.

I'm surprised, and look up at her in astonishment. She smiles and says yes, I am calling you from far away. You are my Sister.

I wake from my trance, amazed. A dolphin from the Amazon River was calling me, and she claimed me as her sister.

The next morning a note arrived from the Post Office: I had a parcel to collect. I didn't think much about it – I couldn't recall any parcel I might be expecting. Later that day, I went down to collect it. Oh! I'd forgotten I'd ordered a crystal, shipped all the way from Amerika. When I got home, I opened the parcel, expecting to see the crystal of my visions, the round one with rainbows in the bottom I had visioned and then seen on the web. The Earth Grid crystal was there, but another also accompanied it.

An Atlantean laser wand, used to call dolphins. I gasped in astonishment. It seemed that my near proximity to the dolphin crystal – even though I didn't know it was there – had helped me dive deep into the magic cetacean world. It wasn't the first time the dolphins had called me, but certainly the first time one had claimed me as her sister. Why that should be, I still don't know: Sister, will you come to me in my dreams?

Once upon a time I had lived in a house right beside the Yellow Sea. From my window the ocean sparkled, and the fishermen went out every day, in their ancient rowing boats. One evening I strolled along the promenade. Grandfather Whale: I saw you come!

How surprised I was to see this magnificent being arrive through a portal in the ocean. Straight from his Star, Grandfather Grey Whale came. He was enormous, so lengthy and huge. His presence was extraordinary. He had great sight and commanded all.

How he could travel! I watched with awe as he sped the speed of Light across the Pacific to the shores of southern America. Around Easter Island he paused, and did a dance, inviting the spirits down through the empty, unused monoliths. On he went to the coasts of Chile, where he called pods upon pods of his kind. Cetaceans all, dolphins and whales, came to hear the Grand One speak. I saw him charge up for air. What a magnificent site to see, amazement like none other in all my lives. Tall he stood, pausing in midair, splashing back down with a tonnage force. And then he was back, mid- Pacific. He held court there, mending the tracks. The sonars were confused and scrambled. Only Grandfather Whale could sing the true sound. Sing he did, till he righted the grids, enormous relief flooding the bodies of all cetaceans who had felt sickened by the confusion of the grids. Now they could sing their own tune again in concentric circles of delight.

As all was well in the oceans grid, Grandfather Whale bid his farewells. Dolphins and whales alike jumped high as they could, foam splashing around their glorious bodies. Then Grandfather Whale made his swift spirit swimming, back to the Portal in the Yellow Sea. And up, back, to whence he had come. So portent had been the arrival of the Star Whale, that even the heavens heralded it.

A thunderstorm was threatening the clear afternoon skies over Qingdao bay. The Yellow Sea was moving with turbulence. After a few thunder rolls, the pretence of a storm, an unearthly silence, a great golden light infused the heavens. There was something of an eerie quality about the air, the horizon was blue-grey and misty, and a pale goldenness pulsated from the west...

I'm drawn outside to breathe in the sea. Ahoy! In the distance I see the dolphins dancing. They are doing a dance of greeting and welcoming, a Great One is due. The dolphins out to the deep sea do a circling, nose to tail fin, nose to tailfin. They form a ring, and are in slow motion moving with the waves and the breath of Earth, the ocean tides, round in a circular motion, swimming and breathing in solemn circle. The welcome dance is for the Great Whale, he is coming from afar, to manifest in Gaia's oceans for a while.

Oh! He is here! Splashing in the center of the dolphin's welcoming committee.... His body is huge - of a kind rarely seen on Earth - an unusually large and long Grey Whale, with barely any encrustations on his back: such is his manifest power. Grey Dawn has work to do in the Earthly sphere, a changing of dynamics, a recording of the manifest points. The spiralling impulses manifest through tides. He is overseeing electric changes in the Earth's oceans. He is infusing these points with love. The electric points are small atoms in the water molecules. By this infusion Grey Dawn is assisting a change in the balance of the seas, a change from fear-based energies propounded by the humans, and specifically the military-minded humans, who are want to discharge negative-charged ions into the sea.

Grey Dawn is romping with the whales and dolphins and will travel many seas, bringing a trail of light sparkles behind him in the currents. Beings of Light and wonder descend to honour Grey Dawn and to assist in the integration process. Grey Dawns' travels start from manifest Point in the Yellow Sea and will form a spiraling circle across Earth's Oceans, from one side of the Pacific to the other, before returning to Stellar Source.

Afterwards, I had returned inside, and felt the earth move. A phone call came soon afterward. There had just been an earthquake nearby – in a town that rarely is bothered by them – and it was a 5 on the Richter scale.

Later, I heard them call again, the wise ones of old, our cetacean playmates of the wondrous times...

We swim, we swim. Now and then, in the old earth and new, we master the multi-dimensions as we play in the seas. We anchor the sonic waves as we move through the waters, for the Light codes can easily enter your oceans. Fluid, they are, gentle, like a baby's breath. Specific strains of information are located on special stones underwater. The stellar codes come blaring to our world, and you, the humans, hear not. We know the places and the keys. The timings of our migrations mimic the stars. We dance in the surge of oceanic grace.

The sonic codes are the road by which we travel. Over the many eons of our lives on earth, many are the humans with whom we have played. We love your gentle natures, your kindnesses, and the sound of your laughter is like the twinkling of little shells. When you laugh, you are in Grace, and the sonic waves may reach you, if only you would listen. Long ago you built temples in the special land places, places where you could hear with ease.

The special places were made of a certain type of rock, its vibration such that the waves could flow through them, and be stored for a time. Like resonators, transmitters, these land beacons echoed with our thoughts and stellar light. In the ancient times, in the times of Mu, we would play with you, there. Many of you would come, in communion with us. We remember those days, those days of glory. So many of you waiting for us on the beach. The slow sound of the conch, played by one of your experts. How close he came to making the dolphin mating call! How it amused us and cheered us, but we said not a word. For then the singing started and you joined in all to make the one note. The one note which resonated throughout the galaxy, the one note of peace and love and universal stillness.

The many humans on the beach, making this haloed sound, caused a vibration so great the world stood still. And in that lull, some of you disappeared, down the halls of time. The time-travellers returned, usually on the next full moon, and the groups in circles sat around to hear their tales. What wonders and sorrows the futures held. We the dolphins have known all along, that you would return soon to the days of old, and hear our voices in your dreams. There was a time when our Star-Elders called us home. When the pollution, the thickness and ugliness were paramount upon this planet and the very sound we emitted caused sickness in our brethren upon our home. We came a-surrendering to the inner spaces, our multitudinous beings merging into the few, so as to make the journey home. For thus we had arrived, before the dawning times. Many bodies merged in the few, to multiply though the dimensions once sure and certain, once the few had checked the viability of the new planet's oceans. The oceans here delighted us. So glorious is the world of your sea. Why do you ignore it so, and treat it with such circumspect?

A shallow stream led through the rocks. It was in the time of Mu that we swam up this channel. One at a time, or in threes or nines, we entered into the island pool. Together with you, the Lemurians, we swam. Oh how joyous were those days! Humans and dolphins in the inland pool, melting and merging into the group consciousness. Together there we prayed to the Stars. It was our ritual, the rite of home. Honoured we were the humans came. Some in spirit leapt on our backs, and made the journey to the Motherland. An underwater world, so full of grace, from which your myths of mermaids stem: that is our Homeland in the Stars.

Some of you stayed, reluctant to return, metamorphosing into mermaids in the stellar worlds. Your King Neptune was one of those. A human cetacean blend of consciousness, he settled into his role well. He never really lived amidst your seas; instead he reigned from our home world, yet his presence was felt on this planet, stern and profound.

Ah those days of aquamarine wonder. They are coming again soon they are here! For we are the multidimensional ones and we straddle the time frames with ease. Now we are here in your warming waters, now we are here in the new earthstar. The new waters bring us much delight. And you, the humans, with the wisdom of eons, like the ancients you were: yet now you are with even more light. In the new earthstar you are shining bright. A negative thought is not permissible since it would colour your aura so much you would drown in it. And the oceans you have made, again with us! How we delight in it now, swimming with those of you who have transformed. Whoever could have thought it, from the olden days, that mermaids would come to play on this planet? But come they do to play with you, for in actuality... They Are You!

Some of your kind, the human kind, will transform again, into aquatic ones! What beauties you are, with shining smiles! Your children lead the way, for they have no fear.

And the songs they sing are of such joy new universes compound in the outer space.

We the dolphins await you now. Long have we stood beside you as custodians of this planet. Long have we played with you. All along we kept the matrix running, through our sonic beams of Light. And now you join us, in our sacred work. For this we are grateful, and so very glad. Long live the new Earth, in your words of old. For we have seen your hearts, and know they are divine.

Seaflower

In the ancient times, our spirits danced, danced like we did on the stars. Eons ago, in the Lemurian lands, we floated on the ethers across the wide seas. Our bodies were made of flimsy and thought-form, our desires of love and grace.

Long ago on the stars, I planned this journey with you, my beloved. On the star we planned our song. In the warm golden heart of our stellar matrix, we sang the seasons and the dance emerged.

Tonight I recall our precious dance: how long has it been since I remembered, how much of our souls have I forgotten? You give me a gift in the calm of night, when children sleep and the lights dim. I see a bird, a large white bird, and you ask me do I remember. What great sadness overcomes me for a while, when remember I do not. Then the visioning comes, fast, spontaneous eruption; I am with you again in the times of Mu.

We were together then, beloved mine. Our souls gently travelled, flying over the precious lands. It was the early days, our bodies so light, our spirits inhabiting them easily, with grace. We shed these tall physical bodies we had taken on, a light form of matter, to fly as we once had, in love and elegant form.

No longer did we travel the stellar pathways, now we were earthbound, and we flew over the Grand Pacific. We took in the beauteous nature of earth: it was a delight to see, an impeccable beauty. Flying was different here. Our light-bodies were heavier, so we took some time to renegotiate flight. We had to accustom ourselves to this strange gravity, which seemed at first like a heaviness pressing down upon us.

By the time of this story I am about to tell, we had grown into this earthly life. We were earthlings now, one and all, and were used to circumnavigating the islands of our dreams. Honoured One, I hardly know what to call you, knowing you as I have in so many different guises in so many lifetimes, using so many different names. Honoured One, my beloved who is also beloved of me, the names matter not, naught in the scheme of things. For reconnecting with our souls is our journey now. You are my beloved and I yours for we were so in the beginning times, great streams of Light, Gold and Silver, complementing each other in perfect grace.

Dear reader, you too are of the Light and Grace, you like I descended into the thicker realms, the material planes, to blossom this Light and Love and Grace into worldly form. So grand it was, my love, your love, all our first soul loves, we sort only how to clarify its beauty in expression. Express ourselves we would in the denser planes, so our love took many rainbow forms.

Alas and alack, we forgot! We forgot the greatness of our original form and became hung up on karma and the acting out of dramas. Throughout the ages some of our partners followed us, companions in time and space, lifetimes of togetherness trying to find true expression. Bitterness and hatreds emerged in the dark. Some of us, some of the beloveds, parted, lost in space, unable to reunite. A daunting nostalgia overcame us, those ones who were aching, all the time, for their one true love. Eons of solitary struggles encapsulated our lives, those of the beloveds who chose this path. From the heavens another soul looked upon us, calling out, calling. Oh, we of the negligent ears! Others became lost in density, friends and lovers caught up in separate dramas, taking lifetimes of karmic to-ing and fro-ing to unfold. Our elders told us to follow form. To obey and not question. To live in the society constructed by man. Arranged marriages, falling in love and out again, all collided in an ephemera of patterning we termed reality.

The rainbow forms had emerged. We could not have known they would include such victorious pain. Those days are gone now, the days of pain and misunderstandings. Only Love, only Light, is our now path. Like the days of old in Mu. Recovering our long-ago soul partners in love is part of the journey Home. Come with me now, dear reader, as we journey again.

I came tonight to tell you of days of old, yet got lost amongst the grids of the new. Like a flower unfolding in bliss to the sunlight, the new world is opening before our very eyes. It comes with memories deep and strong: for the new world is to rebuild the days of old: the new Lemuria upon our shores. But for that, it is true, I hold no pen tonight. Tonight it is the wee hours, and I am to tell you of dreams. I am to tell you of dreams of love, love so grand and spontaneous it spanned eons. Eons of lifetimes of incarnated forgetfulness.

Ah, dear reader, so close to me tonight through the wefts of time: Alas! Alack! Abracadabra! The spell is unbound and we are here, together, now, me as I write and you as you read… dear reader… do you know of such love? Yes, yes you do! Such love is inside your hearts, now and always.

Let me tell you of my beloved. Let me tell you of my dreams. In my night vision I saw a large white bird, appearing in front of me in the nocturnal dark. Whilst children slept and the lights dimmed, the white bird, I know not of what kind, appeared. Surprised, I stared at it. It had appeared out of nowhere.

"What message do you hold for me," I asked.

"You don't remember? You really don't remember?" I heard a voice say, and I sensed the energy, the presence of my beloved. A deep sadness overtook me, that I could have thus forgotten. Then it lifted, the veil gone, and I saw, was back again…. floating…

great spirits we were, floating beings of ether. My star-love was with me. We were floating in currents of air over Mu. Over the seas we drifted. When we stretched our spirit-bodies, large we were, loose fittings of atoms melding into consciousness. We were light and flying. My beloved and I, one stream of light. Yes, it was, you were with me back in the thence. Often we would fly. Our "bodies" so light, yet still denser than spirit. Easily we could seep out of our bodies, and fly, fly, like in the days of old.

With great reluctance I am drawn back. For how can I describe the beauty of this time? Would that I just remember, again...

In the air our silver spirits melded, grey auras of atomic light. We glided over the islands and oceans of our home, seeing below with the eyes of the winged ones, how beautiful this planet, how glorious to be as one. This love we had, so natural, so grand. Our spirit bodies joined and entwined, floating in the currents of earth's air. Our love so natural we joined with such ecstasy.... from our passion and love and communion, a white bird formed.

Ah! A miracle of remembering, how could I forget? From the wonderment of love and natural merging, a white bird, a giant one, formed in the sky. In her passion and joy a white feather dropped.

The white feather dropped into the oceans, and floated, floated, to the shores of the islands. Someone found her, this White Feather, and took her to a temple, where she rested, rested... and became a source of healing to all.

70

White Feather was thus birthed, as had been her matrix birthed and planned in the stars from whence we had come.

Others of you all, dear readers, have stories as grand as mine. Let me tell of them here. Yours? Or yours? Raising your hands in the circle of our remembrance, dear Lemurian kindred, who is first to speak?

You? Our thanks. Here is your story, your brow anointed with the golden oils of earth, amber sap from the ancient ones, the trees standing in the grove yonder....

I see them come, all glistening golden, your skin taken with this colour of the Sun, as you marked your path as the Solar Lords. Commune you did with our saviour, our Light, the Blessed Ancestor who shines every day from the east, who causes our food to grow and our world to have colours and light and wisdom. As a solar lord you wore a lion's mask, and you chose your beloved from amongst your own rank.

The Solar path was a natural one to you, since you came from the starry gates in the sky, where you were incumbent in a Sunstar of your own home world. You knew the mechanics of Fire and Light. You chased the atoms and brought them together. You held consciousness with your council of five, for five was the sacred number of your space. Entwined you were in solar light, in this Star of

71

your first home.

Your beloved now in the lands of Mu, the graceful homelands of the first-formed earth, was also a Sunstar solar lord, who came from your home star. Awake you came, in ships, in spirits, to this our new home. Awake you knew your beloved's name. You had taken new form; you delighted in the play of your new bodies. In your home worlds you had studied well. You even had a playground simulating Earth, so the gravity wasn't so surprising.

Beloved, your name was a whispering sound of light. Eventually, it became known in the English words as Teresa. Galiath, your soul was claimed to you: your name choice in Mu was resonate of this sound. Galiath. Teresasashha.... Beloveds, you swam in the oceans, the dolphins your dearest friends. The delight of your love was your play in the sea. Every morning you swam, every morning you loved, the air above a spiral delight, a funnel of rainbow air formed from your love.

Who above, dancing in the rainbow spiral, its form like a typhoon but of no such severity, could know it was the union of your delight which gave birth to such beauty? For you swam underwater, for ages, like whales. The dolphins were your perennial playmates. You sang with them in the midst of your desires of life. Only those who knew you well, who too surged underwater, knew that your melting into the atoms of each other caused joy bubbles to flow upwards in the sea, merging with the air and creating the rainbow funnel. Sea-flower, we called it, this multicoloured spiral of breeze.

The birds gathered, feeding of this joy, playing in the rainbow shadows. Their songs joined in your submarine moans. Those of us on the hill were transported to bliss, at one with the spirals of air. Inside this bubble we created our own dreams, and as we floated in the rainbow torrents we dreamed of games to play and delight to invent: a new song, a new instrument, a new dance in this world.
Your love was grand and strong, but not unusual. This was the way we all lived, in these days. Love was the most important of all, our joy, and our reason to be. How could love degenerate into shame? What crazy world did we create in the after-times?

Teresassshhhhaaa. Galaith... thankyou for your dreaming. Who else would speak?

Oh, tis you, sweet sister of the southern realms. Clad in the garments of the north this time. I see you sitting on your swing, streaming grand braids of Light with your dexterous hands. This is how you played. Sitting on the fairy swing entwined with flowers, your hands a dance of Light. As you weaved stars were aligned, planets calmed and storms abated. Your hands were mysterious wonderings and could conjure up little miracles for all who watched. The children loved to sit by your feet. You were not far from childhood yourself as I recall. A young maiden with your train of babies and children, the younger ones had grown up around your feet. Even as a child you loved the little ones, and as you grew, so did they, remaining your dedicated assistants and loves in life upon lifetimes to come.

Where did you come from, Sister mine? I see your sweet smile and feel the sweet fragrance of your breath as you rock back and forth on the flower swing. Oh! You have grown now, and he is here, your chosen one. Oh! He is one of the little ones grown tall, younger than you he grew under your spell, knowing nothing but love for you since his earliest days. You too loved him, like an elder sister, until your love blossomed into the growing seasons of time. Onto your swing he comes and sits, but he knows not how to weave with his hands. This you teach him, patiently, till he grasped the rudiment of these motions.

Then it is he who weaves the basic motions, holding the matrices still whilst you weave more subtle rhythms, he sets the existent patterns in the starry heavens so you then can build grand stations, constellations whirring in the breeze, stardust in your eyes, flowers in your hair....

All this upon the swing, with subtle movements of the fingertips and hands, like yogis and bodhivistas. Suddenly you realise you are in love and your souls stretch and laugh; for you knew each other from the beginning of time. Sister, you walk off with your love in flowing robes, you walk into the gardens and palaces divine with hands clasped, you bow and pray in the same motion, you complement each other perfectly in heavenly union.

It seems that everyone has seen the golden swan, swimming on the lake in the evening. The swan seems to appear only in the evening, and some only glimpse her magnificent wing of woven gold. Others, the lucky ones, watch the swan glide over the lake in glorious serenity. No-one recalled when she first appeared and no-one knows from whence she came, nor who might have co-created her.

Sister, your blessed union with your soul partner brought joy to our world and smiles to all. Was the Golden Swan your gift of love? Or someone else's, hidden in the breeze? Or did the swan appear of its own accord, navigating celestial winds to appear on earth? Cygnus roams in the night sky, as the golden swan's appearance was fleeting.

Our dreams in the ancient times made our beautiful realities. We dreamed of things not yet to come, they appeared before us in prescient beauty, as we tread lightly on the earth. Think you, dear reader, of this: wherefore is truth? It happens that you think, perhaps, my tales are but fanciful things of allegory. Stories to comfort you and help you sleep at night, words full of the lull of a cup of warm cocoa. Maybe, be that as it may, but my stories to you are also the truth, literal truth from the days when co-creation was as natural as breath. Today it seems like some grand magic, something we would love to be masters of yet can't, something left for children's stories and not relevant to adult lives.

And could not grand magic reappear on earth? In fact it must, and it is. Grand magic is the natural way, manifesting our dreams in the physical plane, dreams in harmony with our Earth and Sky, dreams of love and abundance.

My tales of love are as true as I know. Since my dream, white feathers appeared everywhere. Today a white feather floated down to my path, as my little friend and I walked and played. She walked her toddler steps down large rock stairs, and there, the white feather floated into the descending evening. Yesterday I bought a present for my friend, and the shopkeeper wrapped it in paper of midnight blue, in which white feathers were imprinted with glistening light.

What tales of love comfort you in the night? What love story moves you as you walk through your days? The great spirit love illuminates our earth-walk, and as we find our way home, tired after a long day, we walk past all our past loves and present, to find the one and only, true soul companion. Sometimes that one has chosen density and trials: what can we do but send our love from afar, and move on. Sometimes that soul is around us in spirit, too grand to incarnate in this still dense plane. And sometimes that soul is beside us in life, a life partner of love and grace. Whereever, whence-ever that love may be, walk past them we must, and acknowledge. On some level we merge, in the bright light of the soul. And if we can stay together with that love, there is no greater bliss on earth.

In Lemurian days, Love was love and we merged and matched in a myriad of ways, soul essences come together to experience bliss on this planet. The bliss emerging from twin souls embrace, created majesty in a myriad of ways. The golden swan glided on the lake. Whose swan is it, dear reader, is it yours? The golden swan is all our loves; she comes to glide in our dreams, bringing us truth and majesty. She tells us the truth of our true loves. Dare you dream? Dare you manifest love in your lives like the times of old?

Dare you not, dare you not...perhaps this is the better question. There is no fear existent any more. I am White Feather, a gift of love created by myself and my great spirit beloved. I am the spirit floating across the seas; atomic grace emerged in the presence of my beloved. Lemuria is alive in our hearts and souls, our true Eden upon Earth. It was before, and is again. Lemuria was a place, where we once lived in grace. Yet Lemuria is so much, so much more. Lemuria is a state of mind, how we live our lives. As Lemuria rises, again we find our place in the sun. With our beloveds beside us, and All is Well. All is well.

Weavers of

Time

Amongst our brothers and sisters, there were those who played with the faeries in the flower realms, those who communed with the subterranean crystalline world, and those who cavorted with dolphins. There were also those who delved into the fascinating scintillation of time and space, as they danced their magic together across the universe and cemented the formation of clumsy bits of matter, the best of all pleasures. These ones, our brothers and sisters, spent their days and nights in the temples of meditations and the halls of the hilly lands, where they lay at night communing with the stars. "*Wu li*", one branch of this science became known as, the dance of energy. The English word for this dance is "physics".

These brothers and sisters, brave ones and true, held the matrix for our lives. By power of thought they kept wild atoms and random molecules in tight formation. Because of their talent for dimensional travel, their forms can still be seen by those with sight. Some never left, some kept guard from a far-away space, and some simply made the great jump-leap from then to now. Of all the things I will tell you in these pages, these time-travelling nymphs will be the most hard to believe. Fear not, scoff not, let your heart open, and your body rest gently, deeper, onto this our solid earth.

Time is a swirling vortex. It doesn't always leave us where - or whence – we should be. Few are the ones who know how to navigate its spirally gravitational force. I am, of course, no time-lord, just a woman with a traveller's tale to tell. Back in the then time, when no-one had heard much about the healing power of crystals, I wrote much of this story, and more. It came out as a fairy tale, of those wee ones living in the underground realms, who used crystalline lasers to heal great wounds. By the power of intent and focus the healers would send the light of the lasers into the deep wound of the material body, and without much fuss, molecules would leap over molecules in a swish of elemental *qi*. Cells would be cured and alive with new blood, which would in turn infuse the matrix of the physical body.

The timelords occupied the spaces between distant galaxies, and when they greeted us, on the body of Gaia, wrapped in physical form and speaking our language, we hailed them as the majesties they were. Pray tell us, sacred folk, of the times to come. Tell us of what you have seen in the pathways of the stars. Talk to us they would of what they wished, bringing great wonderment to our eyes. A boy or girl, enraptured by such marvellous tales, would sit by their sides, and disappear into dust as the timelords moved on. When they returned, the youth would be clad in gold and wearing the signature of the timelords.

For long eons these kindred of ours danced in the stars. As we became more and more incumbent upon our material bodies, they danced with more dedication in the realms of pure bliss. They held the codes for us to reawaken, and never did they forget their sacred duty. When the matrices of the "old time" broke, signaled by harmonic convergences and harmonic concordance, they started to reappear in our visions. Some called them angels, some called them deities, others labeled them stargods or spirits of a lord, yet who were they but our own long ago folk, the ones who chose the realms of time, to work with and play in.

How wondrous that you return to be seen in our time, you who were always there, weaving the threads of the grand reawakening. How fortunate we are you stood by us, through eons and eons of our self-made unfolding dramas. Did you weep galactic tears at our manifest follies? Did the blood of your beings rise in disbelief, at the atrocities we invented, at the hatreds that raged?

Time-weavers, of our glorious past and futures, we give you great thanks for your patience and love. For without your dances, holding the matrix throughout time and space, how could we come to this great crossroads in time? How could we reinvent ourselves into our true natures? You held true to us, when we didn't know our true selves. Your hands were made of pure beams of light, and with them you recorded our lives in great loops of infinity, figures of eight of our own lost selves.

And now infused again with galactic light beyond our Sun we can see your movements, and thus remember our futures and rekindle our pasts. Timelords, wondrous weavers of time beyond our knowing, we bow to you in gratitude, for you are our souls' own grace.

The

Changing

Times

There was to come a time, in our perfect world, when all would change. Underneath our gardens the crust of earth heaved. The seas leapt in high waves, strange tides washed up against our shores. We knew it was time for the Great Renewal. It had been forecast; we knew it in our very bones. Some of us had already left for the Western Isles, and we had heard little back since their departure.

At night the mothers mourned by the sea, waiting for their children, the brave sailors. They were not to return, would not return, all knew that was the risk. Could we contact them by our usual means, telepathy? No doubt some could. Others sent their dreaming bodies out at night, to return with tales of splendid domes and large cities beyond our imagining. We were at heart an agricultural people, communing with nature as we went about our lives.

The fabled cities of the Isles of the West attracted many. Unheard of glories, priests with powers beyond our imaginations, cities that gleamed majestically in the sun: it was the stuff of myth and legend, except then we did not know what myth and legend was. Our society then, and the Atlantean ones, were the first to create myth and legends, paradisiacal isles in the dawn of time, gods and goddesses descending to earth....

But the tales, nonetheless, were enticing ones, and entice they did, a good many. Of the first to go were the adventurous type, or the scientifically inclined, those who wished to observe nature in another place, under another sun. And there were those for whom love left little choice, craving the company of the atlantean sailors who ventured to our shores. We had had priests there on our isles for some time, the atlantean ones, with their wands of crystals and their long robes. They visited our temples as they first arrived. They built their own quite enormous structures. Marvels to behold, out-shining the natural wonders of the world. The boy called Kofv was enamoured by them, for days he would sit outside their walls, swaying to the chants that emanated from them.

An elder, pitying him, spoke to the priest, the chief one inside the temple. Take him as your own, the elder had said. Train him in your esteemed traditions. Look! Can't you see how he pines for your knowledge and how he reveres your gods?

And so it was the boy Kofv was taken soon on a ship to the Isles of the West. With him went chaperones, singers, scribes. With him went the counters, the classifiers, the joy-riders. As the first ship sailed out we all stood on the beach, watching, waving, some sobbing, some cheering. We all knew then the times of change were on their way.

A few more ships departed at dusk, in the months after the first ones had left. Earth was changing with this new adventure. We could feel her underneath us, rising with heat. The plates were scintillating, vibrating in an edgy rhythm.

The waves continued to roll; large, shocking waves that crashed with such voracity on the sand even the birds were scared. Knowing a great earthquake was about to erupt, the first of the immigrants prepared to sail. For now we would all become immigrants. No longer a matter of choice, a journey to the Western Isles had become inevitable, since the quake would soon destroy our islands. We could feel Earth purring underneath us, rumbling, moving, waiting to erupt.

Many left yet some stayed, staying till the very end. Little contact was made with those who had gone, as all our psychic strength was needed to pacify the earth. There was no time or energy left to telepath our kindred nor for distant travel in the times of sleep. They would wait for us, this we knew, prepare our new home and welcome us with joy when we finally arrived. For of the leaving, there seemed no choice. Not many stayed on till the very end. The promised land was awaiting, and our islands were doomed. Many who left had left their hearts, buried their treasures in the land of Mu, to sink with her when she went down. This was their act of love for our homeland. Special crystals, experimental diagrams, sacred flowers and drawings, mantras and mandalas, so many lemurians gifted their love for Mu, by leaving their treasures in sacred earth. Mu the Motherland knew, and held the treasures to her bosom. The names of those who lived on and left the shores of Lemuria are written in crystalline code. Those who love her shall be given a chance to be reborn upon her beloved shores, in the new world, the world of joy.

There is so much I am leaving out of the tale; so

much I prefer not to dwell on. The traces of panic did appear, for the first time in our civilization, in this the Changing Times. I left I left after the rest had gone. Some Lemurians choose to die with Mother Mu; others like myself made our last farewells and set sail. Some left their bodies, by now denser than before, and flew to Atlantis, blossoming again as the new generation. They carried Lemurian codes and memories and grew up to be priestesses and priests.

And now my tale must take a new turn, one I am reluctant to take. Yet down this road I must travel for it is the path we took. I remember not much of the journey nor if perhaps I left my body to be reborn again in the New World. All this is faint.... and unimportant. Let us just say I drifted into Atlantis, the Isles of the West.

And wished I could drift right out. What I found horrified me. How could these people claim to have a civilization like ours? How could they be doing the things they were doing, the genetic engineering, the near-to almost slavery, the animal compounds. How it grieved my heart to see how they had trained the crystals. And "military"? Who had heard of such a thing?

Already the factions had formed. The Lemurians and the pure Atlanteans, who wanted a return to the old ways of peace and harmony. On the other side were the technocrats, who had their plans all in place. I walked the streets in search of my old friends, in search of the old ways. I entered the temples to pray and to find peace. I tried to go underground, in my spirit, like days of old in Mu, but the entrance was blocked by fierce dogs. Who? How? Why? So many questions boggled my heart. Why would they block the underground, the shimmering zone of minerals, a home to all. And then I saw one night in a dream how they were digging and destroying our friends the crystals, tearing them from their homes and setting them against alien minerals, with no thought of who should energetically be next to whom, and in this morass added electrical impulses OH! I could hear my minerals screaming, the awful shuddering of crystals as they were shattered by high-pitched noise.

I look in the blackness of smoke rising and shake my head with sorrow. Something has gone wrong, totally wrong, the whole matrices of earth have been altered, become unbalanced. The dragon energy had been harvested and set to work. Precious crystals became jewelry, ornaments for the powerful. The bigger and more radiant, the more power to show off. I would send out a ray of sympathy to the crystals I saw hanging round such people's neck, and the crystal would shudder for a moment. They became cloudy in such a role, hiding their shine.

Long I traveled with an elongated face. I ran into friends, relations all, from Mu. Some I barely recognized, yet I knew their spirit. The changes upon them were unfathomable. I did not understand how they had become how they had become, forgetting all proper behaviour and ways of life. On the other side of the mountain lived the wise one, and I was told All would be revealed by her, the story of what had happened to the country and the people.

But I could hardly get there. Before I had time even to consider leaving, more dramatic events took place. Some of the creatures had been let loose. They rampaged down the tree-lined streets, growling at those who dared to come near. Horror more than fear entered my heart. Shock, great shock, as I watched them gallop mindlessly, up, then down, the street.

A soothsayer came. I recognized her by her long black dress, lined with gold. The people, who had been cowering, stood upright again. The sounds of whimpering hushed. I heard feint voices, whispering. She had come from the temple of Zoltaran, this much I knew. I could tell by the metallic circle she wore around her neck. It clung proudly to the rising of her breasts. She worked some magic: she weaved the old symbols in the air. The old ones, then the new ones. I knew the Atlantean symbols well enough, as I'd seen their priests perform at our temples, back upon Mu.

A few of the fiercer dogs had surged towards her, but then a gush of lightening came from the sky. A tall figure emerged, from where, no-one could say. He seemed to step out of a cloud, I was watching – or thought I was – all of the time. He must have been hiding behind her, of course...or in one of those back-alley shops. Or behind the trees, or.....

He was dressed from top to toe in royal blue, and the robes were embroidered with stars. At one sight of him the dogs ceased their bark. One, then two, had a rush of bravado, a few growling steps forward, then back again. As the closest creature to the magician dropped suddenly to the ground, apparently lifeless, the others backed up, and ran away.

A hush came over the crowd that had lined the

streets. Then out of nowhere, one clap toned... another... till a great applause echoed down the streets. But when people looked for the magician, to congratulate and thank him, he had gone. Only the stooping figure of the woman who had preceded him could be seen walking slowly away, southwards. No-one thought to follow her.

In the beginning times, Atlantis had technologies of pure heart and beauty. Precious crystals were used for healing; temples of sonic grace were maintained by the Priests of Sound. Mantras of divine intent sounded with the song of conches and the vibration of taut drums. Gardens of structured beauty: long lines of rosebushes, flowers matched by colours and size; and stone brocades along the wide streets that led to the seaside.

Atlantis, islands of the west, your name has become one of intense mystery. Through the ages, memories of your greatness, and your excesses, haunted our dreams. Civilization did not forget you. And now we seek to find you again, we wish it so that we see you dressed in finery, standing beside your Pacific cousin, holding forth the pure and true light of crystalline wisdom. No more shall we speak of the strange times, all memories rusted in time, dusted with the breeze of ages.

Atlantis, once you shone. Civilizations beyond worlds were intrigued by your majesty; beings from the galaxy and beyond came to learn in your famed schools. As we gather in the moonlight, to remember Mu, our arms are extended to you, our kindred, to come together again, and play. No tale can be told of Lemuria that does not mention the name Atlantis in it's telling. For the two are linked, beyond space and time, beyond any magic to destroy.

The two words, the two civilizations, were the beginnings of polarization on earth. They mark the original split from which all others were patterned, protestant against catholic, Islam against Christian.... Why does this word "against' pop up so often in our histories? May we erase its memories and it's curse. May we live henceforth united, Atlantis AND Lemuria.

Golden Rose

What, you may be asking, does an island from ancient, mythological times, have to do with us today? What meaning can it possibly have for you or I, with our busy lives at work and play in the 21st century? More than history, more than myth, more even than some forgotten fairy-tale left to rest in a tattered child's book in the attic, Lemuria shows us a way of Being. Lemuria is a way of life, a way of doing things, a way of living bravely, beautifully, with ethics and a warm heart. Lemuria was a time long ago, but it is also a place in the heart. Lemuria is a dimension of the soul, an unforgettable part of human existence, a trace memory and root experience of humanity's time on Earth.

How do we recapture it? How do we know how to live like the ancients? How can we possibly be the same, we who have lost faith in magic, and don't know how to dream?

Do we wait for an island in the sun, to shoot up out of the darkened seas, in the aftermath of some tsunami or tidal wave? Is it the land we are looking for, bathed for untold eons by the blue pacific? Are we searching for magic stones and ancient temples, where dolphins once prayed alongside humans? Or are we trying to find a better way of existing, on our patient, bounteous planet Earth?

How can we create, like the Lemurians did, wondrously, joyously, in honourable partnership with our planet and all her grace her shores? We know so well the many mistakes our humankind has made over the currents of history; surely we don't want to repeat the madness that erupted from splitting the atom. If we say no to this, and to genetic engineering and gene-spliced foods... where do we go in creating the new? And what is the difference between creating new species in the way the Lemurians did and the madnesses of cloning and genome technology? The difference, dear reader, can be summed up in one word:

Integrity.

Integrity. With integrity, one cannot harm others. With integrity, one cannot harm the planet on whom we depend upon to live and breathe. With integrity, there is no way we

102

could consider causing so much damage there would be naught left for our grandchildren and future generations. The Lemurians lived gently, with love and grace for all around them. When they created, they did so in conjunction with all who shared their space. The Diamond and the Rose were co-creations, both bringing great joy to the people of Earth, and to the magnificent planet-being Gaia herself.

Can we live like the Lemurians? Can we be as them, again, after so much we have seen and done on this our long-suffering planet? Doubt it, you do, you with your mobile phones and your trillion varieties of television screens, you are thinking this tale just so, a tale. The deeds of the past, the future possibilities: do they lock you in torment, or give you cause for strong emotions, pleasure and grief? Our future is as we make it. This is the Lemurian way, the Lemurian life. To make our futures together, co-operatively, hand in hand with Gaia. Her flowers, her stones, her rocks and crystals, her animals, four-legged and two, her birds and her bees, her every nook and cranny, mountain ranges and valleys, beaches and bays, her underground layers and hollows.

To create, again, our dream, our paradise: that is the heritage of Lemuria. What would I weave, what would I dream into existence, if again I was back on the land of Mu? Better still, what would I create on the new earth, where the ways of Lemuria will once again reign supreme?

To sleep, to sleep , perchance to dream, a famous poet once said, yet our Lemurian cry is WAKE! WAKE! To wake, perchance to dream...

On my new earth is a Golden Rose. It is of such beauty, such radiant grace, it is almost indescribable. But describe it I will, as it will, with your help, appear in our new earth.

There are no brambles on the rose of the new earth. Few have thorns either, unless we should so desire. But you are familiar already with roses of old, so I will not continue with them, nor compare. Our colours are different, here, in the new earth; our two suns create such a vibrancy you wouldn't be sure where you were. The light, the very atmosphere, is golden.

We are walking down a path, and everywhere beside us are flourishing trees, greenery everywhere. The trees grow like an arch, over the quiet path. Pennyroyal, or a soft grass which caresses the feet, lines the path. It rarely needs mowing; it has enough sunlight to live and enough shade to not grow wild. Through the overhanging vines the sky is clear. Out two suns are shining brightly, and little rainbow circles fly around the atmosphere.

I'm walking to the Rose Grove, its one of my favourite places. There are many Rose Groves, but this one is on top of a hill, overlooking the bright sea. With a breath of excitement I glide up the hill. It always excites me, this method of transportation, cause it wasn't always that easy to get around on earth. My feet are taking steps but my soul is flying, and my body, no longer weighed down by the weight of the world, can move so fast my feet can step on air a few inches above the ground, if I so choose.
I choose to do this now: I want to reach the top as fast as I can. I want to see if my new baby has taken root in the soil where I planted her upon the last new moon.

The moon has waxed and waned and is new again tonight. Already a faint sliver hangs low above the ocean, I watch her with joy. Moon, moon, is my new tree a-growing? Yes dear, yes dear, your new moon's a-growing. Moon, Moon, is my new tree a-growing? Grow she will, grow she will, the new moon's a-growing.

I'm on top of the hill. I pause to look out over my love, the grand sea. We call it the New Pacific, after the old Pacific Ocean. It's a beautiful, shining twilight, and will stay like this for days. A lavender-blue tinge to the air, a cool breeze tingling our skin. Oh! I see it now, my new shoots! They are delicate things, raising their green heads to the sky, on the edge of an established bed. I bend to tend and water them, there is water nearby in a small brook and water in my pail I have carried with me. I sprinkle the gem remedy to help them grow; I sprinkle some water over the little buds.

The shoots dance a bit, tingling with the breeze and the cool liquid. They will grow, they will grow.

Others have grown like them, but this time we want to see what the sea air of the New Pacific will do to them. I sit for a long time in meditation with the ocean, the sky, the roses. I walk amongst them, the orange ones, the white, the red and yellow. The large ones and small, the tea-roses, the china-roses. All are here, perfume floating around the evening air.

Three moons later, we are in the Rose Grove. Another Grove, amidst the gardens of the grand white crystal house, the place where the crystal workers sing their gems into life. We are watering, we are tending, we are singing with the roses. We are dancing, we are playing, we are living with the roses. We are giving thanks to the flowers for enriching our days, our eyes are grateful for the glorious sight, our noses pleased by the fragrance. In the atmosphere we can see the fairy devas come to play. They

106

dive and dance, following etheric roads between the rosebushes.

For those without extra sight, it seems like a majestic dance, choreographed and carried out flawlessly. For those with the sight, the faint roads of air can be seen, glimmering like fairy-dust in the sunshine. The sighted see the devas tiptoe along the roads, fly down the long avenues flapping their devic wings.

Sounds like the twinkle of angelic bells fall effortlessly into the day, as the devas and fairies flap their wings. All is well.

Another day, a secret valley, bushes lined in outlaying circles, criss-crossing the grass. My smile is clear and full, quick to come in this place. Closer to the trees, the fruit is visible, little balls of gold, luminescent and scented. It's a fragrance unlike any other, and it leaves you heady, breathless even, till you become accustomed to its rare scent. The balls are deep gold, sparkling in the sun. They are not glary, they don't cause the eyes to gasp and pale from their glow. They sparkle, enchant, delight.

Getting closer, someone takes one in her hand. She doesn't pick it, she simply sees what it is like to have this radiant ball briefly resting against her palm. She is filled with calm and joy. To others watching, it seems as if she has taken on the golden aura of the plant, just by touching. Others step forward, and still others. They touch, look, commune with the fruit.

Don't eat it! says one mother, as her child has swiped the fruit of the tree in a quick motion. You can't eat it, says another, playfully watching the child.

It's so beautiful, says the child, I just want to look at it.

Alright, says the mother, but don't pick any more. It's the fruit of the tree, the tree's baby. It's a looking tree, not an eating tree.

Oh, says the child, Oh! It's so beautiful.

Rainbows dance around some of the fruit. They are different types of fruit, some with skin a pure shining gold, and inside others, rainbows dance.

Look! There's a rainbow gold one, someone calls out, and the others say yes, look at the rainbows dance.

The little balls of gold and rainbow gold dangle voluptuously from the trees. There are only these trees in the secret valley, the bushes with the fruit of gold and rainbow gold. I smile at the delight they bring and I am enchanted. That night, as the others return home, I sleep in the valley, amidst the roses. I dream strange dreams, of other worlds; I hear the dolphins calling and the woman of crystal. The woman of crystal has spoken to me before, she exists only in the Dreamtime and she visits us all. Our Grandmother, she speaks of the times to come and the crazy days of our pasts. Many don't wish to recall the troubled times, but others insist on telling the children, so they will know, and not go down that way again. There is a history school, far to the back of the village, which records the dark past in photos saved from the Great Fire times. I don't go there, I have no need: that history is etched into my memory, and for the most, I have forgotten its details. It does not claim me anymore for our world is new and golden.

Crystal Woman brings with her the Golden Rose Girl, and I bow to her in greeting. Golden Rose Girl tells me she will give me one flower for my vase in my room, and I bow to her again, in thanks.

In the morning, I see a whole tree with flowers in bloom. The rosehips have lost their hardness and grown petals. Gorgeous blossoms of pure gold abound. A few have even fallen off the tree. Golden Rose Girl, knows me well, I think, as I never pick the first flowers off a tree. The tree must be blooming, and ready to drop naturally before I will take the flowers from their mother and sustenance, the tree. I smile again: overnight Crystal Woman and Golden Rose Girl have given me a flowering bush, past its prime. Flowers have already dropped off and are scattered on the grass like a golden carpet, while the other bushes still hold only rosebuds.

I walk to the bush and stare at it in wonder. This bush never ceases to amaze me, these perfect flowers a miracle. Thank-you, rosebush, I whisper. Do you have a rose for me? I put out my hands and the bush bends in the winds. A large, multilayerd rose touches my hands. I'm overawed, as this flower has the rainbows on it, and not all do. Are you sure? I ask the bush again. This flower seems to for spectacular for me. The bush sways again in the breeze. The breeze is so strong this time that the flower has almost become detached of its own accord. Sure, I hear. I touch the stem towards the end of the rose. It's delicate, ready to snap. It seems just by my gentle touch, the stem has broke, and the rose and stem have fallen to the ground. I pick it up with care.

I see Rose girl again, for a fleeting minute. Her hair is streaming as she flies off in the wind. Thanks, I call out in my mind. Thank you, Golden Rose Girl. I walk home slowly, holding the rose by her delicate stem. At home, I have the perfect vase, made from white quartz crystal and given to me by the carver of gems. I find the purest spring water and *put it in the vase. Reverently, I place the golden rose in the water. Rainbows swirl around the petals, vivid, bright colours. Inside the bud, is pure gold. I have a miracle in my home.*

It will of course, bring me dreamtime visions, or waking ones for that. I meditate with its energy, and I'm taken back to the trying times.

Back in the here and now, I smile again. The thought of the golden rose fills me with joy. In the future, as in the past, we shall fill our world with joy and delight, co-create with the nature spirits and Gaia, only what is perfect and natural upon the shores of Earth. The oceans will roll, the dolphins will play, and the glorious songs of birds will charm our days. Crystals, crystals everywhere abound, of all kinds and colours. There are crystal houses too, shaped out of pure stone and willed into existence by the gem-people. They share their world, of course, as it is so beautiful. An amethyst cave as a meditation studio, a glory of emeralds on the stone road, and quartz, dearest quartz, you are everywhere in our dreams. The castle on the hill houses the ruby crystal; we take turns to accompany her, as in days of old. No longer does she shine in the tunnels underground, now she has come out to play. In her glory she sits on a table of white quartz, in the castle on the hill where the children play. Ruby, my ruby, thanks for being in our world.

Reader, dear reader, thanks for being in my world too.

Let's join hands, a hug even... go on, no need to hesitate, yes! That's it! A warm bear hug and off we go to create our new world, where golden roses bloom and dolphins dance with us every day, our Lemurian home has come again to stay. Come! It's time to make our new world, in our dreams and our every waking days.

All is well. All is well. All is well.

contact the author....

at

www.dipperstarlight.com

www.ingramcontent.com/pod-product-compliance
Lightning Source LLC
Chambersburg PA
CBHW031901090426